# Getting Dressed

## Amy Lipman

SPUYTEN DUYVIL

*New York City*

## Acknowledgments

Thank you to the editors who first published some of these poems: *Ghost Proposal, Rabbit Catastrophe Review, Columbia Poetry Review, Pinwheel* and *Ghost Ocean.*

Thank you to my parents, Bobbie and Jeff Lipman.

Thank you to Sandra McCoy-Jackson.

To Laurie Carlos, Lisa Dixon, Brigit Kelly, Michael Madonick and Matt Minicucci—thank you for your brilliance and generosity. I will always remember the privilege of sitting in your classrooms.

To CM Burroughs, Jill Magi, Tony Trigilio and David Trinidad—thank you for your guidance and for teaching me much more than you know.

To Lisa Fishman, for everything, thank you.

Thank you to Nicole Deter, Rachel Hasler, Traci Hercher and Fae Rabin. Thank you to Annah Feinberg. Thank you to Jenny Christie. Thank you to Jessica Volpe. Thank you to Naomi Stoner. Thank you to Holly Amos, Alyssa Davis, Tyler Cain Lacy, Dolly Lemke, Sam Schaefer, Patrick Thornton, Naomi Washer and Abigail Zimmer. To many more who have listened, read, and written—thank you.

ISBN 978-1-947980-02-0

Cover art by Fae Rabin

Library of Congress Cataloging-in-Publication Data

Names: Lipman, Amy, author.
Title: Getting dressed / Amy Lipman.
Description: New York City : Spuyten Duyvil, [2018]
Identifiers: LCCN 2017044329 | ISBN 9781947980020 (softcover)
Classification: LCC PS3612.I637 A6 2018 | DDC 811/.6--dc23
LC record available at https://lccn.loc.gov/2017044329

# PART ONE

## WALKIE-TALKIES

Tonight

it snowed, it

fell from the sky

and covered the ground,

it fell through the atmosphere,

and the greenhouse gases, and the

clouds and the waves of the radio. I

used to share a set of walkie-talkies with

my next-door neighbor, Megan. She could find

me, on the signal/on the current that was made/born

between our houses, just by pushing ON. After that, we

became immersed in one another, though neither of us was "there."

## PORTRAITS

My mother
sorts buttons
in a small
wooden chair.
Her creations
are not
portraits.
They are
several
arrangements
of many
single
lightweight
pieces.
She
sorts
through
what
she
has
already

and when
she knows
the ones
she wants,
she sews them
through
their
button holes
onto a
board.
I like
to look

at them.
They
make
me
think
of choosing.

# November 7

I wonder how long it will take me to "arrive" anywhere while sitting here

my knees are bent, and so right now, I am shorter

the bird outside is somewhere (around the corner?) and unaware of my listening

I spend equal amounts of time thinking about people I see regularly and people I will not see again

there are a few that got "away"

who haven't left the city.

One is Steve and he lives just up the street, and we keep different hours, so we don't come and go in any way that intersects or even parallels one another; in fact, I suspect that our separate movements are rarely significant or productive at the same time of any day, but this is only what I suspect, and this suspicion is only probable & within the realm of truth if he is at all the same as how he was back when I knew him.

## Your Shirt

I haven't been invited
to see your new house
and this makes us
even farther away.

I miss you and miss your big feet and I miss you,
I miss how you sound when you're driving and miss
how you take off your shirt like the guy
on TV who we laughed at and
also I miss you, I miss you in the way
that butterscotch barely exists
anymore and also
you won't
give me back
my bikini.

## YES, I WAS OK

The *apple* I brought I caress quietly in my palms and that done
immerse myself and take a bite
My teeth take a bite and the apple's vermilion rind tears smudging
faintly its soft-snow flesh
One bite another, and at the *apple's* sourness I tremble faintly in the
morning bathtub
—Okamoto Kanoko, Bathing Body, 1925

*

Never having experienced a bath like Okamoto Kanoko's, I feel
unprepared to fully experience this day and the ones following quickly
after it.

If I could, I would ask Okamoto Kanoko if she was expected to bathe
every morning.

I feel more for the morning than I do for the night.

Upon waking, I bend all of my toes at once and then release them.
Then, I sit up and try to get my neck loose, letting my head be heavy
as it makes imperfect circles.

In acting class, Lisa talked about the horizon. We were to arrive at
8:30 in the morning to the orchestra rehearsal room, dressed in loose
clothing, on Mondays, Wednesdays, and Fridays.

She walked in and we got up to stand and make a few rows, with our
eyes forward.

She wanted us to keep our eyes open with a soft focus.

She came around to make adjustments.

She tried to make my shoulders loosen.

I apologized but maybe she didn't hear me.

My mother was so careful with me.

Yes, I was ok with baths as a child; why confess the rest of it?

The water wasn't warm enough and I always liked hot water, but when she put me in the bath, we just looked at one another.

## NOWHERE IN PARTICULAR

I need to talk on the phone and nobody answers the phone

When the phone was attached to the wall, that part of the home was important and often in use

Now, the phone is often kept in a pocket but taken out often and checked before it is put back and then taken out of the pocket again

If the phone is on a wall and it rings, we go get it

If the phone is wherever we go, we go nowhere in particular to talk

## December 15

This building is very long—it goes back, moving west, and the walls built to nod to the north and south face each other and they stay 10 feet apart. The east and west walls, in my estimation, are 50 feet apart. You can see that the room is not a square. Its emphasis is on length so that makes it a rectangle.

In the back left corner, there is a green 7UP machine. Next to that is an industrial fan, turned off, because it is December 15 and it is cold. The vending machine holds a few bags of potato chips and then row after row of Milky Way. The TV is on and the news plays. They say today is the busiest day of the year at the US Post Office. Just underneath the TV, there is a green cord with small jewel-toned bulbs hanging from it and the bulbs are lit up. The man running this Laundromat watches over his space. He scratches the lower half of his face and wears a knit hat.

Two boys sit in the middle of the room. One goes out of the Laundromat and then there is one left. When the first boy comes back, he carries two white plastic bags. He pulls out a tall green bottle made of glass. San Pellegrino is inside the bottle.

The TV now plays *Wheel of Fortune* and a contestant excitedly shouts "Two Is!" There are two dings one right after the other and she says, the pitch of her voice ascending, "I'd like to solve the puzzle!" The puzzle mentions an apple.

To my left is an arcade game. The name of the game is Ms. Pac-Man. I remember playing Ms. Pac-Man in an arcade up north with my sister. For no more than two hours on one afternoon, we were inside the arcade with one another, selecting games on which to spend our nickels. This was an afternoon just one year ago, so we were adults, and we had plenty of nickels. We didn't have to ask anyone to give us more. The arcade was called Nickel City. We saw some games with things that spun around and lit up but we kept mostly in the back room. The games in the back only cost a penny. That is where we saw Ms. Pac-Man next to Pac-Man the original. My sister and I stood next to one another, commanding the movement of two digital blobs at our respective stations.

She moved on to several levels which I never saw.

I stayed inside of the same screen, chomping through the dark.

## The Ones She Liked Best

When my mother took me back-to-school shopping,
the extent to which we shopped depended on
how much I'd grown out of the clothes purchased on the last shopping trip
for the previous school year. There was a consignment store
she really liked in Hinsdale and it took us almost 40 minutes to get there.
On Saturdays, we went to garage sales, but
I just wanted to go to the mall and pick some things out
and go home. I didn't want to try very hard.
I didn't want to sort through many racks of faded clothing in someone's
poorly-lit converted garage and determine the pros and cons related to one
piece of
clothing up against another piece of clothing. Neither of them were right.
These clothes would be what I'd wear at school for the next year, at least.
It was so hard back then to decide if something "fit" because I kept
hearing I'd soon grow, and that even if I purchased something
meant to fit me in that particular moment, that eventually, it wouldn't fit
anymore.
And this was stressful, too, the idea that my growth was out of
control, and that the extent of the spending of another person's time (hers)
and money (hers)
depended on trying to select objects that would accommodate this
unknown, unwelcome factor.
And yes, if something was full price and she thought it made me look nice,
then she would buy it. For example: we once saw a rack of denim vests
at JC Penny with patches of satin-like fabric
accenting the vest in certain places.
We approached the vests and they looked even better up close.
I said that I did not want a vest but my mom said
that she really wanted to buy one for me,
but then she bought two.
I still think about
how nice those two denim vests really were. I felt, back then,
I was unworthy of them. They were for me
to wear in fourth grade, on fall days, over turtlenecks. I had two

turtlenecks
and I had two vests. One vest had a red & pink heart
on the back; the other had a black & white star. In a photo of me
wearing one of the vests (the one with the heart on the back)
my mouth is totally closed; it is sealed tightly
and I'm smiling without teeth. I still feel badly—
my mother spent her money on things
for me. And I hated some of them,
which were the ones she liked best.

## T-Ball

Our t-ball game ended early
and since we had the field
for the rest of the evening
Rachelle and I played leap-frog    left alone    jumping
she crouched with her head tucked
and closed her eyes    I straightened my elbows at take-off
mostly straight up        I went    but then I        leaned forward    to land
and closed my eyes, too    like her        hearing all the people in the park
maybe they weren't watching us    still, the carriage    the sounds
a sunset & someone mentions it    dogs    bat-and-ball        someone
drinking through a straw
while I was up there    it felt very important    to have reached a height
made
by the arch        of another girl's form    wouldn't someone    feel proud?
Then, my gum in her hair    couldn't remember    having opened my
mouth                                her mother    got a comb    was very angry
I said    maybe if we add some water?

## WHAT I HAVE MADE

Greeting cards
One ceramic pot
One jar, filled with Karo syrup and plastic stars, so that the stars could
move slowly through the atmosphere of the syrup when somebody turned
the jar over with their hands; over meaning upside down or diagonally
slanted or over itself again and again, as in a rolling pattern
Trenette
Linguini
Pappardelle
Tagliatelle
Pici
Orecchiette
Farfalle
Lasagna
Ravioli
Pesto
Bread dough
Bread loaves
Shapes in the snow with my
       foot
       feet
       finger
       palm
       whole body at once
Half of a puppet (abandoned the puppet halfway through making & then
lost track of it)
A fort
A room to be spooky (within a haunted house)
A few different versions of mashed potatoes
Juice to drink in the morning (from squeezed oranges)
Cakes for various occasions

# December 28

I walk past the Laundromat tonight and it's a suitcase full of dirty clothes I pull but I have just stepped off the plane about two hours ago and it is too soon to make these clothes clean. First I need to step into the house. I need to step into the house before I do anything.

## February 22

I possess a kind of health
somewhere; I know it.

I come awake each day like this;
right away to talking.

## GUACAMOLE

I crush a soft green fruit

my hands are so       happy to feel

the inside of       a commodity,


I see the      little spine
    dollhouse of      the jalapeño,

      I want to rely

    on my hands      and what they make

      but I need      so much

&     so much     else

## Going To Get A Ginger Ale

It is sweet        and it soothes the stomach.

I am convinced that I need to be soothed.

I go to Red Star Liquors, which means getting out from under
the blanket

opening the door, locking it behind me

and seeing half the courtyard bright and half of it in shadow.

Walking north toward Schubert Avenue, hoping to see Steve
again like I did two days ago

when I waved        but had to call him over because he
didn't recognize me.

# SILENT NIGHT

In the process of learning the song "Stille Nacht" for the fourth grade
Christmas Pageant at River Woods Elementary School, I was curious
about the meaning of the German lyrics. I asked the teacher what
the words meant and he said it didn't really matter what they meant.
All that mattered was that we were singing "Silent Night". Everyone
already knew the story.

The words, individually, did not matter. Nobody told us exactly what
we were singing with the use of the words of the song. Everyone
already knew the story and the story made them happy. The reason
we were singing the song was to commemorate the holy family and
the holy birth, and the reason that the school had us sing the song
was so that we, the children singing the song, could enjoy the journey
of singing it for a rapt audience who also already knew the story but
wanted to hear it again.

In the story, a family does their best in a situation that is less than
ideal and then they all become holy.

We also sang one Hanukkah song and because I was going to Hebrew
School at the time I knew the meaning of many of the words in
the song and I put together a rough translation for the class, after
being asked to provide one. As in every language, in Hebrew there
are a few sound combinations that are difficult for many people to
pronounce if they have not grown up hearing the sounds regularly. I
tried helping the class with the sounds but they mostly laughed and
became embarrassed by their struggle to pronounce the words, so the
words in the Hanukkah song were not pronounced correctly and so
I think that, by this logic, much of the German song must have been
mispronounced.

Like many other Hebrew songs commemorating events in Jewish
history, this song was not as much about the events themselves as
it was about the ongoing significance of the events. The words of

the song emphasized the importance of <u>remembering</u> the events, and why the events should still be considered a triumph. The events were not enough—nobody was singing about their love for the Maccabees. We were singing about remembering that the efforts of the Maccabees mustn't be forgotten. Nobody has much to say about the positive qualities of the Maccabees. Jesus, however, is celebrated as an individual with appealing characteristics.

When I explained to the class the events that took place which prompted the establishment of Hanukkah as a holiday, the other children seemed unimpressed. I don't like explaining Jewish holidays to people. It is rare that somebody seems like they'd want to join in and I can understand this—I find most holidays to be a letdown and I'm not even very interested in my own birthday or in the birthdays of other people. I acknowledge birthdays and have a good memory for them but do not feel that they should be celebrated in an extreme fashion. However, I will admit that last night was my birthday and I felt disappointed by the actions of someone who had previously acted as if birthdays were very important to celebrate in general, which prompted me to invite this person to spend time with me on my birthday. He said yes; yes, he'd come to meet me, but then he was late. I was upset while I was waiting for him and I was upset when he arrived. When he arrived, there was somebody with him because he had invited this person to come along, but I wanted the two of us to spend time together without anyone else there. When I explained the expectations I'd developed and my subsequent disappointment he explained that he consistently disappoints those around him when asked to do the following things: 1. Be on time 2. Recognize special occasions.

According to this person, he consistently misses the mark; he shows up, but with the wrong company or in the wrong clothes or with the wrong thing and/or at the incorrect time. After thinking about his comments, I told him that it is better to attend an event than not, no matter who is going to find fault with one's style of attendance, but right now in this moment after further consideration, I remember that what is so soothing, after all, about being an adult, is making the choice to stay home at night.

## THE TRUTH

The truth is, she died a year ago
and I am just now feeling sad
not because I did not know that she was gone
but because I had not thought of all the things
I had not known about her
and do not know, and will not know, even now
that her things are making their way to me,
such as her record collection;
I did not know she had one
but yesterday, my father
who lives far away from me
(we live far away from one another)
came over with a crate of her records
(for me to keep temporarily)
after helping to clean her house.
The crate is blue and plastic and the property of the *Chicago Tribune*.
She wrote for the *Chicago Tribune*
and now nobody who writes for it
is someone I know
and I know nobody who
subscribes—
my parents subscribed
and I read that newspaper every morning.
Sometimes I even carried it up to my room if
what I wanted was a quiet morning, keeping to myself, reading the news.

## GETTING DRESSED

My father's t-shirt        with the stains

      it says "Pop Art!"        there's a picture of        champagne.


The last time he wore contacts, he was

in the bathroom                before work

and I was getting ready        for third grade

      walking by in the hallway        on the carpet        as
                                           he told me

to watch him put        the contact in.

      I was so                proud of him.


And then, when                Christopher Jamrose,

      the fifth-grader,

didn't know        how to get the

pepper seed out of his pupil,                I said

"like this!" and touched                my eye

and he said                "how disgusting!"

## You Are Far

The radiator comes on
and you move close to me.

This far from the water,
there is nothing that instantly calms me.

You are far from water, too.
You are right here next to me.

## TOMATOES

At Marshall's, the department store prices      were reduced   and

you could bring a high number of items into

the fitting rooms     One dress     among so many  that I chose

to try       green silk   the first thing     clinging  to me

*

We brought them home and       peeling back sweet paper

of the ears    white kernels   some the way that butter looks

when it is shaped     my fingers    worked and brother  sat

on the grey steps     dropping husks into    a paper grocery bag

and the corn silk

*

My brother lived down the hall from me     he played the trumpet

when I learned to ride a bike    it was late

there wasn't a bike for me     at home    so I borrowed

one belonging     to a neighbor

*

Becky Troast was our neighbor  she swung on   the swing next to me


Her yard had the bigger hill     Mine had tomatoes

*

Becky's lace curtains and my mom's white couch

their wooden table and ours was glass
they went to Kansas     not us

each time she went
back to her home        from mine
she was            skipping

I watched it

*


Before bed—
towels            tissue paper     colored pencils            thread from
hemming

but my
comb
have you
seen it?

Michael Jackson glove from my father
Dorothy and the Tin Man from my father
Checkerboard from my father

I asked mom to leave messages

in a basket outside of my door;

I wanted anything that she wanted      to tell me,

what she didn't think of while we were together      during the day,

and so      in the morning      I received

"bring me your laundry"

# Quiet And Slow And Dark

Right now it is Christmas Eve. I know that Christmas Day is coming and that, around me, nothing festive will happen, but that others are counting on the day to be the day throughout which many wishes are granted.

Here, in the late afternoon, I know that there is much ahead that will be quiet and slow and dark, like the sun setting and dinner being prepared without a lot of focus, and I look forward to that feeling with all that I have right now and with all that I've held on to through this morning and afternoon.

One Christmas, we lost my brother's iguana. It got loose in the house and we looked for it. We could not find it anywhere. We didn't see the iguana for three days, so we started to forget how it looked. By the time it came back, we were startled by its presence, since we had started to adjust to the idea that we'd never see it again. During the original iguana's absence, we purchased a new iguana, so then we had two of them, but we didn't need two. We didn't think that it would make sense to try to return a living thing to a store, even though it was true that we had purchased it under a return policy, so then we had two iguanas for a few years. They did not get along and they had to be separated. They lived separate lives but we still thought of them as a pair, in alliance with one another, because they were so different from us. However, it is true that the two different iguanas liked the same things; they liked the dark, and eating, and their electric heat rocks. They lay on the rocks without moving after they ate so that they could receive aid in digesting their food. Often, they lay on the rocks at the same time, but in separate rooms, without seeing one another.

After eating, I take the dog out and then I usually sit down for the rest of the evening. What do you do? I worry that my table manners are deteriorating, since I often eat by myself. Before I ate by myself with such regularity, I lived with my immediate family in a house and during family meals, my dad said I ate very slowly. Back then, I had to trust him because I hadn't seen enough people eat but now I have seen many people eat and I know that he was right.

I wondered, when I was in elementary school, if it was possible that I was very, very stupid. My classmates moved around quickly and loudly and several things happened as a direct result of their actions—noises were emitted, objects knocked over, there was motion, and dust or dirt occasionally became visible in the wake of their motion. But I sat quietly, deliberately in one spot at a time, and I liked to read the same short books over and over and I always felt surprised when anyone said my name; when anyone had a question for me or wanted me to get up and move closer to them. When anyone would call me to them or think to ask me for something.

## SEEN FROM MY BEDROOM WINDOW
## AT 813 CUMBERLAND COURT

When the streetlamp came on in the evenings it was around 6 PM, mid-November through February and something like 8 PM, March through October. Where light was needed in between was not attended to by the city's streetlamp schedule and when the lamp went on and I saw it through my window I also saw that it went on not because of anything my parents or my brother did—whose is it? I asked my mother, and she said It is the city's and then, every day after, when I walked by, crouching down to run my hand around its base—it felt like stealing and I loved it.

The bicycle that I picked out at the school rummage sale laid on my front lawn at the end of the summer; Monday through Thursday it stayed in the garage but Friday through Sunday I used it every morning and every afternoon and so I was permitted to lay it in the grass and one day my neighbor Megan took the bike and rode it, because her lawn became my lawn and because she was two inches taller and her jeans became my jeans and because she learned to ride a bike before me and now that I had a new machine to add to the neighborhood which was very small, which didn't include our whole block, which, to us, only included our two houses, plus the ones on either side of them, she felt and I felt that to pass the bike back and forth made sense because we needed to know exactly how the other one was functioning and at that age there were not many questions        concerning mystery     that we could articulate and so our only understanding of each other's separate lives came through in the way we needed/stole each other's possessions.

## CARDINAL DIRECTIONS

A new phase of my life began
when I learned
how to name

cardinal directions.
Once I knew I could
trust myself to determine

which way I was traveling,
I felt like a legitimate part
of something;

even more,
I felt
I could finally

provide
factual information
with clarity

and confidence.
When I was
sixteen,

I lived in a suburb
without obvious landmarks—
there was no collective sense

of a body of water
or any natural elevation,
although, within the town's limits

there was a building
which we all agreed
was the tallest

and also,
we had a bell tower.
Now, what helps me

to keep living in Chicago
and navigating
is the shared knowledge

of the lake
and also
the tallest building;

being able to say
what direction they are
from all points.

Anyway, at sixteen,
I was to begin driving lessons
and my father first wanted me to learn

to read a map.
I agreed that this
skill could be helpful,

but I did not
think it was necessary
to learn navigation

before I learned
how to operate
the car.

His request made me upset;
I cannot know the right way to find a place
if I haven't first been permitted to move.

So there we were,
my father and I
on the phone one night

when I needed him to pick me up;
I gave him the address
but he wanted directions.

He asked whether to go
east or west
on 87th street

and all I could say was
"down"
but when he asked again

I said, "you pass the church, and then
you'll find the street
and turn right."

I didn't know why
he didn't get it.
I waited for him for a long time.

Finally he arrived,
but for all that time
I had been waiting in the same spot

and he had been
driving
around.

Sometimes when people
are late
to meet me,

I forget to picture them
traveling to where I am;
it begins to feel that

out of the two of us
I am the only one
without the other person,

and that the other person
has all the freedom,
and that because I am the one

waiting
and trying
to be patient,

that I am at
a loss.
It starts to feel

like they are out
in the world
being active

and I am
just saving
our spot

and that if I am merely holding on
to something,
I am not doing anything,

and that it is only
when they arrive
that I will finally have a reason to be there.

## Do I Deserve

this blanket
photo of Acapulco
small jaw
cedar chest
Polaroid photo
birthday party?

Do I deserve this bed
my health
and all the rest?

I bought the mattress
with the help
of savings bonds.

I left work early
on a Thursday and
walked to a strip mall.

Once inside the store,
I tested every mattress
by briefly lying down

and the salesman,
impatient,
asked me what I wanted.

# PART TWO

.

# NATIVITY

I am the one who takes the extra stuff,

that's why I have

an abacus. An autoharp.

And an XL green turtleneck and a framed peacock.

Some of these paintings are by my grandmother.

She painted lilies

a tall blue woman

some abstract forms

and my sister.

Though I never met my grandmother

she is here, in this apartment;

there's the small statue

of a queen, holding a basket

and inside of the basket are some rhinestone cufflinks

and at the foot of the bed there is a box of glass animals.

There's also her ceramics;

the nativity,

the ashtray.

## THE WALK

I walk and I have walked
in every room of the house, but it is that

"why did I come in here, anyway?" feeling, which does
not put an end to the walking and then

I get an apple to eat so that
I will have something.

# A Radio

Green Grocer across the street

Burger Baron next door

Manny's Auto Shop adjoining

we must be careful

not to get swallowed.

We with our kitchen

me without money

room full of flour

&       yes,

a radio.

## Potential

There is a part of the wall against which

I pressed my hand throughout last summer

when I wanted to feel something cool and low,

like the ground.

Now, still inside,

I want to get warm

and the warmth for the room arrives through a vent.

I consider the seasons

and which people I see in what season and

realize that you are someone

I reach only

occasionally,

so there is not a lot of natural potential for closeness between us, but

my tablecloth

is clean

and folded in the drawer

and in a home with breakfast, lunch and dinner linens

there is potential for closeness and more—

who will fold and press onto themselves the napkin that I give them and

will they love

what is for dinner?

# April 11

I am seated in a chair which is sitting on linoleum and a man standing
near me holds a prayer book in his hands as he looks at its pages and
then rests the book on top of a gumball machine—with this action,
the book is still and unhanded while the man mouths the words as he
stands next to his book and I notice that his prayers are work; I watch
the words as they're made and spoken and once the body is at work,
all touch and meaning coming from it also needs direction/effort
and we choose to move along  with or without devotion.

## April 12

I just slept. To my knowledge, I lay still. When I began this particular night, my diary was next to me but I had no use for it as I have decided recently to make all of my routines just slightly different and then neglect to record them.

Before, when I was hungry, I ate an entire meal seated. There is, of the food, no real evidence. It's like it never happened. As soon as I rose from the seat, it was over.

# A NUMBER OF THINGS

I remember about you        a number of things        and the longer we
stay out of sight of the other     the things I remember     disperse
and they find somewhere else to attach          and remind me of you
unexpectedly

so when I make a list describing your attributes and possessions
I know it's incomplete because of what was then unknown and what,
within and around you, is presently     changing
I liked so much about you then          that I could name        but still,
it was hard for me to explain     just what it was        I liked that salt
on the table           I liked how you left it there after it fell while we
were eating      or while we were preparing to eat        and in the
morning I could trace it with my finger          make it move    and take
some with me under my nail

there was an orange light        I could see from your window    the light
was positioned at a height somewhere which was          higher than the
roof of your building and        its position, I believe, was distant
          I didn't know          but I saw it; part of it            in the
evenings          and I keep it    unfinished and not fully seen
alongside my lasting     image of you          which I cannot
keep     from changing

in trying to remain a full figure          throughout your many shared
abstractions     I sensed the promise    of a number of days     after
which you would make          a decision about me     and I
kept up my      normal bathing throughout the dry     odorless process
of waiting

all the dirt     I smelled on you and    tasted        and all the dirt's
origins: garage and bedroom    where you worked     the yard and
walks during which you'd start to sweat on your own

the senses aren't reliable        they're flat until        someone
walks in


it can help to write a letter        uninterrupted  wrist and fingers
words

you and I sometimes were good        but I'm having trouble now
without        am I responsible        for the ongoing absence of
the good, and noticing, and making something of it; the growing
amount that I want it back?

how much do I want    when do I receive        I imagine many
things        many times    without making an effort        to
really    get        throughout a day        having a vision creating an
expanse        open mind        letting the mind build the vision
and        falling into what I make in the mind and staying willingly/
often

## June 10

I challenge the perimeter by looking around, all around, where there is nothing to "see."

# DREAM

Where did you go in my dream?        I know where you go in real life

but where in the dream        which was mine

could you have thought to go?

## Alphabet

Ascending the steps
barely containing any clues
correct all invaders and be sure that they
do not pick anything up or put it down.
Endings are a
fear of mine.
Godly camps among the country road can tell me to listen if I'd like a
light held in
front of my actions;
high-ho
it is good to go and work, but not even fair and/or
just thinking can reach one answer, so
let us pray for
mother to travel more widely; she has
now used all of the
offers to be taught new things, and not through reading, but through
interactions with the
people she knows already.
Quietly I
reach for the grain I will prepare for dinner this evening.
Stay for dinner, I want to say, as soon as you wake up, and luckily,
to ask for an outcome like shared time together
unifies the asker and her desired within a shared
vision of togetherness, but just for a moment, because we have to ask:
could
we could stay together for a whole day?
exact
ly. let us not rush into thing-
s.

\*

As soon as the cake was ready you can
bet that I be-
came very hungry and
does it matter to you that
every day I want sugar and
find that
good times of mine
have some element of sweetness? But
I like bitter
jokes;
keep telling them. When I
listen most thoroughly, it is for humor. In
many of my history classes,
nobody spoke
out about the oversimplified
presentation of the
quality of life
regarding each human's possession or dispossession of the four humors.
Still, I remember
them. One about phlegm, one about anger, one about
understanding and brain functioning, and the last was more
vast than
what I could understand.

*

Adding to my list of
basic needs—
corn, squash, beans
down the hallway, the long wooden floor of the hall,
estrogen can't be measured unless I am
fully voluntary and I
go to a doctor and take tests.
Hiking
in a dense forest/finding a frozen pond/drinking from a bottle of
juice. Juice comes in a bottle and it is full of vitamins, what good is vitamin
K?
Lie down
my
new
other;
person with whom I go through days, various gradations of
quiet.
Really, it's because we listen that some of the noise can stop.
Suddenly all of the
textbooks across the room
unveil themsel-
ves—
why is it so
extraordinaril-
y
uneasy in here, when we have all we need?

# Health

At some point, I went into the stable.
It was a place of extreme health, where
all large beings were attended to by smaller beings.

The smaller beings had more external resources and money but
the larger beings had more strength and they were more physically
impressive, in general.

The stables had nothing electronic inside of them.

They remained lit by light and all activities that took place within the
stables depended on the energy of the living thing carrying out the
activity—

the energy,

the energy and the determination,

the energy, the determination, and the level of interest held by the
being carrying out the activity.

## CANDY WRAPPERS

Tree-top

holds the frame

of one        empty window.


Bet         sadly         that

the neighbors

        and their      root beer parties

did this

as     a joke.         Why

else        place

so out of reach

a thing


        that lets us look?


Does it make them         feel better,

      like         throwing candy wrappers

out the window      in a town         you hate?

## The Greatest Pleasure

In the scene far away in the field this evening a group of people played with two dogs and it looked like fun—of course, had I approached I would have gained more of an understanding of the way that everything was progressing and would have known for sure if people were having fun but it all remained far away and my understanding was really just an assumption and so my feelings remained the same.

Here was a group of adults together, under some floodlights in a baseball field, watching two lively dogs run after one another. The group's activity for the evening had at first been merely conceptual; an idea at somebody's suggestion, but now it was happening in real time to all of them—far away, I walked with my own dog, he was my only immediate company even though I could see some other people—the group and I were in each other's field of vision and I rarely see strangers from far away and think that I would be happier *closer* to them—I know it would not be my *proximity to* but my *status within* their group as an established and undisputed member which would yield to an easing of tension, and then comfort.

In my fantasy, I would take the greatest pleasure in the moments within the conversation that only resulted in significance and a collective sense of belonging and understanding because of some nuance of language or gesture; a deep sense of familiarity with the members of the group and their histories, all without having to ask any questions.

Earlier today, I met up with someone I don't know very well, for coffee, and we walked for a long time, asking each other questions— he brought an exercise typed and printed on a piece of paper which he'd been given in an Interpersonal Relations in Communications class in college and because of his careful planning and execution, I felt studied and I felt he was listening. One of the questions was, "when do you feel a sense of belonging?" and I answered that I feel a

sense of belonging when myself and the person in my company have
some overlapping history. When I feel that I belong, with another, in
a current situation, it is because something, between us, in the past,
has already happened. Then, he asked if I had to share an upbringing
or cultural background with my company in order to feel as if I
belonged with them and I said no, and then specified that to share
some overlap in history could mean, on either side of the spectrum,
that we had met once and spent time together briefly, or that we have
lost track of how much time, together, we have spent.

# July 14

I can never know a person until they make full use of the alphabet

## TRUMPET

In the cafeteria
in third grade, we all
got to try

three instruments
and then
pick one—

if I had played
the trumpet
and not the flute.

If I had not
moved to
Pennsylvania,

I never would have
learned how to
drive with

hills.
There,
in

the dark,
that's where I did
my best driving.

If I had not
spent every day
after school in

your mom's green
kitchen, I would
have gone home

and sat in my
own. That would
have been fine

and
a little less fun.
I never would have

eaten marshmallows
with bread. I never
would have

had a
little brother
for that long.

I wonder
where he is.
If I

called you now,
would you understand
that I only want

to talk about him?
Then, you were
the love of my life

but he was
who
I worried about.

## MANY GIFTS

I snuck around
my mother's room
and found a bag
of stuffed animals
underneath the sweaters
in her closet.
Then I knew the source
of all my many gifts;
of all my gifts past,
and, of course, the future.

## LANDSCAPE

As it is          from here          everything is distanced
by more steps

and it is not about          weather


my favorite source of light

can come and go all day


I can only wear a watch

the animals outside react          and after that I keep on
waiting

## It's In The Air

How high the moon     &          then some

  happy birthday                    to you.

Slow     gift     this

placement

  of tea lights,

and then          the whole year,

# In Fact

I breathe next to the palm tree with its expensive spine

where did you go this morning          through a lit room      I can
see      all your limbs

if my mouth can keep up maybe I will go for a walk and after the air
that surrounds me              instead of sitting and swallowing
repeatedly despite a lack of contact with the outdoors or new ideas
from anywhere, and then still not getting anything, despite all the
swallowing

you might call me a name and I could laugh if I am in a mood to be
that name   & I really do want to know where you went        but I'm
happy you are here now so I will          settle down

and I will start telling the story I want as long as the side of my face is
in partial light          now this feels good              even if it is
wrong  the telling might come to me in a          peel    or a raised hand
if I were called on        every time      I wanted to speak        people
would really know      but there are usually a good number of us
in a room        people who want to talk        and more        who
don't make one move at all

all clean with joy from the lemon        the counter is spent from the
flat weight from the light brown cutting board with the stains of what
would have been bark had it stayed outdoors through the elements but
now the only element it encounters is juice thank you to the good fruit
is what I say but it does not nod or kiss me      when I busy myself
with its destruction

in fact              the song is in the other room but it comes here to
me and I wish for a room tall enough where I could sing and nobody
would  know or turn down the        height        of my   throat
        people are proud of the love that they   find    and the love is

made through various distances and borders and my voice and my
weight  or what I think I can    contribute      settles into the curve
that the bed can make  since its edges aren't    sharp   the bed is a
fixed shape in the room but your presence can change that      today

I dreamt in another country we did not know the streets and so
we felt it was us against everyone else but our contact/physical
expression of togetherness added to the scenery and also kept us
away from it so we in a way resisted the atmosphere    by being there
and by refusing to separate

and also I do not want to be a wasted instrument       in the
drawer with rust       and no  handles       any day they could
develop       a solution     to soak in      can anybody   name
the instrument       they need?     can we          all      in
one day?        I close my eyes to picture      a place deep
shameless and slick    an oil stain     on the driveway         that
you     in the summer          by arriving          gave me

## ALL DAY

Leaning against the stove

tonight,          and      looking          around          carefully—I do
not

touch a thing    but see


my spice rack    with the bottles

broken mop       (white head detached          from blue plastic pole)

my plastic bag collection


I        raise

my hand

to ask   a

question;        exercising my opportunity      for more
understanding
while in        one spot,
knowing it is time for dinner again,
knowing there's no meat.

Earlier at the store              as I was pacing

there was a man I do not know he was doing the same thing

near the onions; I was also around the onions

and     now I'm home          calming down.

\*

The marrow
of the bell        pepper
under             my thumb.

On the outside:          it is skin

when I approach it               there is thick             matter

and it's familiar, the matter, or at least the sensation that skin is giving way to
something more important, like an organ or core.

There is a core to cut around,

a system   of columns          its middle-fruit and self          extended

*

my hands run  into the walls of the sink

as I wash up

at this level     where I wash          and my hips     push closer

*

These chores are        here;  they stay undone        until  I make
time for them.

They don't forgive because they don't hear me   they don't hear anyone
they are procedures and  they are not alive      I am the one, in this
situation, who is alive            but I feel so close to the work that I do
cleaning and caring for the household objects and surfaces that
help and        hold me        up      all day—

once, I leaned against the doorframe

while going      out

and thought I heard an answer.

.

# LIGHT

For such
a small

house, I
do misplace

the matches
and it

becomes
desperate

when the
window,

slightly open,
undoes

the thing
I just

did.

## WISHES

tying    several knots   in my bed sheets

tossing parts

of what

   I sleep on

to the ground—

when
running away

fails
or
false-starts


        those left, even
temporarily


they
know   it

# HOME THEATER

That power line is over there
and I am all the way over here,
over the fence & on the other side of a window,
enjoying its effects.

## By Risk

There is a space between the bottom of my foot and the floor

when I step onto the floor, an arch

a hill is made of a small space

*

topographically speaking       it has been a very long time

since some line of my making

each day

was risen, by another person, by risk,

with regularity—

when the events of

the past year    lie down in my memory

as a walk

and I walk through the parts    expecting more,
I don't get more

it would feel good
to make a seal between

what has already happened
and now

and to know that there is a barrier
between the two,
but there is not

*

he's fully formed,
even when it is across a room
in which our distance  is established   like here and now
where I can have an experience with space
by spreading out my fingers

because in school we learned, early on,
millimeters, centimeters, and inches

and I can make and measure all those distances

now with this instrument, my hand, my

palm        romantic        to give
room

through the window
all the favored lighting from late afternoon       goes on comes here
because of the glass;      letting it in.
I am inside so often
and behind all kinds of materials and still       when people speak

of being behind doors

it is much more than that, the enclosure—

I do not love this day or house and knowing that I do not love it
keeps me from settling in
I do not love this day or house and so, with my thoughts, I try to
separate from them

I do not love this day or house but I do the work required of them until
I hear a sound that makes me listen to what is going on around me,
wanting more of
the sound of
water running elsewhere in the building.

I bet I can guess where the sound is coming from.
I understand enough about my surroundings to guess,

but this is a place to recognize and name but not slip into
completely/regularly—to resist

# BELL TOWER

worth
and
luck
and
fortune
and
key
and
oak
and
dirt
and
road
and
shutter
and
piano bench,
and
night

*

I grew up with a        straight road

There were no hills

There was just one hill

We used it for sledding,

        summer concerts,

            and the bell tower.

*

After dinner    some nights,

Dad and I        went outside   to the driveway

to hit a         tennis ball.

We only had    one tennis ball, and so        after we lost it,

there was       no more tennis.

# August 14

the arrangement          of things

all things          in relation          to

one another


the older objects          unthreatened          their own
forms

their own qualities, yes          next to more recently made/obtained
objects


the arrangement, the placement, the order, it's a comfort          to
move them in

to and out of    and in to          their places


the arrangement and order

the placement          the lighting     the day          the order
the month          and season

the accompanying but ultimately unknowable atmospheric
conditions


some of my possessions don't get regular attention,

but when I meet them

unexpectedly   because I am lower down          or at an angle or in a part of the house    I don't think about,

I like them and want them all over again


the name of a material  which is  clearly printed and
all the occasions

of pressing  into it

then, when I fall asleep   to the material  more
happens

whom up close do I know

whom every day do I know

who is known  from our kept and fashioned distance?

and more than this  who else


do I want  more and  more


at times
it is
best to
let
some
other
thought
take
over

## The Temperature

People outdoors       asking what time it is

there are no walls in this field

so borders and also authority/limits are, for now, absent

absent authority       in the outdoors


\*


My style is to wait, not knowing the time, for something to push me

it gets quiet and I hear nothing

or, just one part is sent? Or a vibration is felt?

In the northern part of Illinois it is possible to reach, within the same amount of time, a large city or a large outlet mall. You can choose.

I can't choose when some aspects of the day are done but I can make decisions about my activities.

\*


I wish that official weather reports
included temperature gradations for each spot
in my experience no report can know it all

swelling weather in the distance

inside it's still by comparison

flattened, the carpet stands under furniture

the furnace is somewhere behind the wall, I think

I've never seen it, I just pay for its energy

and how it runs throughout the house.

Right now, there is a particular view from my building which is apart from the building but currently associated with the building, as it's part of what is going on, looking out from inside of it

the woman across the street is wearing a coat and talking on her phone, standing outside of her own space with her own view

we are within one another's field of vision

I feel the urge to position myself in a way so that I go back to being unseen, since she did not request to be seen by me

at times I painfully resist      very natural      interactions—
even when I am          safe      and, in some ways, in control.
For example,
most of my language for the day has been left inside the bed, which
is the last place I had an interpersonal conversation.

## Dear X,

my kitchen can't sing or do a cartwheel

it mourns                 a carnival

then, the sun         came out and              thought

how nice to see you,              more than that

there is the
whole day through

plus, this
moon & pine

the empty truck bed           can't be left alone all the time
it's best
to drive          to you  at night,

ran into your mom              outside that store       that sells curtains
she told me             you're living in the city

ran into a girl from ballet              in Germany
she said                 the neon         silly putty
is still stuck     behind her bed

in Israel          saw Julia
we couldn't believe              one another.

## SMALL VILLAGE

I just got a call from 701
that's North Dakota
I looked it up
the numbers have been reorganized recently
it's the North American Numbering Plan
I went to South Dakota once
and played kickball in the afternoon

Thinking about it now
I only see the field
when flying     over it    the portrait
of the small village, I can see someone's bedding
blue stripes, unmade

of the trip
wanted surprise
a baseball glove
some hunted lunch

noticing
the pond behind the fence

I hop with      all my weight
and then
it calms me, seeing it briefly, the pond

AMY LIPMAN lives in Chicago, where she works at the Poetry Foundation. She previously taught at Harper College and Carthage College. This is her first book.

Made in the USA
Coppell, TX
18 March 2021